IN PURSUIT OF
BALANCE

DIOGENES THE PHOENIX

ARCHWAY
PUBLISHING

Archway Publishing books may be ordered through booksellers or by contacting:

Archway Publishing
1663 Liberty Drive
Bloomington, IN 47403
www.archwaypublishing.com
844-669-3957

Scripture taken from the King James Version of the Bible.

ISBN: 978-1-6657-3758-6 (sc)
ISBN: 978-1-6657-3757-9 (e)

Library of Congress Control Number: 2023901224

Print information available on the last page.

Archway Publishing rev. date: 03/14/2023

TABLE OF CONTENTS

About the Author vii

Chapter I: Philosophy, Psychology and Religion................................ 1

Chapter II: Love Cards (1997).. 23

Chapter III: Myers-Briggs Type Indicator (1962) 27

Chapter IV: The Enneagram or Nine-Sided Shape............................. 33

Chapter V: Energy/Chi/The Force/Good AND Evil 41

Chapter VI: Resonance or Frequency.. 45

Chapter VII: Yin/Yang.. 51

Chapter VIII: Our Painful Path 55

Chapter IX: OODA Loop 59

Chapter X: Using it all together.. 65

Post Script 73

ABOUT THE AUTHOR

I was the firstborn and only son of an engineer father and an artist mother. I gathered wild-flowers and painted on the walls, I visited art, science, and history museums in the nearby metropolis. I had fish, then a dog that I love still to this day although he was allotted only 14 years with us, and went to sports events with my father while my mother took me to art classes. I had an amazing childhood, despite being molested by a neighbor boy. That damaged me to the core, but that demon kept itself hidden for decades- I realized that I was molested at 5 years old while I was in therapy at the age of 33. I had been withdrawn and fearful most of the rest of my adolescence. What I became was a fiend for knowledge, I voraciously read through novels, watched "Shark Week" and any WW2 history, learned new skills and information quickly, but was always socially awkward. I excelled academ-ically but emotionally I was broken and naïve. When a senior in High School, I applied to a dozen colleges but when all my friends got their acceptance letters back- I had not. I assumed that I was getting rejection letters, so I sought a path that didn't include fast food, as I was already overweight. That's when the recruiter found me, and changed my life for the better. I learned confidence, I learned a trade, I learned discipline. I had been accepted to many of those colleges but I had already signed the agreement to show up to MEPS and was unaware I could still go to college if I didn't take the Oath of Enlistment.

After boot camp, I went to my trade school training (not infantry) and was then sent to my first duty station. I was at first underestimated and assigned to a platoon medium machine gun team as we were an Infantry battalion. When I wasn't at a gun shoot, I was working and then the command noticed my competency and drive. They trained me in other aspects of our trade, and when I mastered that quickly- they gave me more. When the Iraq invasion came, I was pulled from the gun team and given more responsibility. With that responsibility, I was repeatedly trusted to ensure that my different units passed inspections over my decade of service. After Iraq, we were sent to Afghanistan where I re-enlisted in country for a tax-free signing bonus and orders out of the Infantry. I served in a Base Unit, a Tank Company, a Command Unit and worked with Reservists. The years were rough physically and when it was time to re-enlist again my body said no FOR me. I left the service for government contracting in simulations, training deploying units. I did this for eight years over two different simulations devices and four different bases. Contracting paid so well, I purchased a friend's business and when I stopped training others- I ran my store and eventually made a second one.

Despite all this success, I was still not whole-depression hounded me. The reason was that loss followed me: my first divorce while I was in service drained me for years, my second divorce cost me everything I had built contracting, but my third divorce is what broke me- I lost my daughter. I was inconsolable for 9 months, then the things I had been studying to try to understand it all began to connect. I found the answer to every question I had ever asked and would ever ask again. With that relief, I found the desire to share this answer.

The path you are on is not easy nor is it pleasant, but it IS rewarding.

CHAPTER I

PHILOSOPHY, PSYCHOLOGY AND RELIGION

TO UNDERSTAND MY PLACE IN all of the chaos that is my life, I mentally and emotionally travelled the paths of philosophers. It also helps that my son was pursuing a
Philosophy major and I love to encourage him. Like most of you reading this book,
I had the Existential question of WHY!? I was at my darkest and lowest point of my life.
I had ruled out suicide after my first divorce, but this time I questioned my religion and
embraced Nihilism- was Agnostic for three days. I was angry at the world, angry at my
country and angry at myself.

I had been a Deconstructive Empiricist; If I can clearly absorb the information then I
can understand the situation and fix it. In that dark place, I followed "why" to Analytic
Realism; I am tired of liars and misdirection, I will look at the information MYSELF.
I began watching videos from disparate psychologists and therapists on YouTube about
narcissist vs empath situations. If any of you/the people I reference receive this book-
THANK YOU! You were my life raft when adrift in my sea of misery. Those videos led

to emotional growth and relief at understanding what I was enduring. Then I went down the wormhole on types of empaths, types of narcissists to the point that I wasn't getting substantial understanding growth such as when I began. Like every other muscle; the more you work it, the stronger it grows.

My understanding had reached the point of diminishing returns so I changed directions. With Positive Scholastic Skepticism, I continued my self-study of the differing schools in philosophy- which is how I can understand and attempt to convey their meaning. If you're a philosopher you get every bit of what I said. If you aren't, I phrased it so that you probably would understand my meaning in layman's terms. Other languages have much more descriptive words and I encourage everyone to learn a second or third language- preferably with a different alphabet. Keep reading to understand why I say that.

> *While reading this book, it is going to be a wide and zig-zagging path across the globe that <u>you should take breaks on</u>. This book is not a "single sitting read". It has taken me NINE years to amass this level of understanding and clarity after fifteen years of professional training, a decade of which maintained heavily negative enforcement of rules and traditions. When I reference some concept or speaker you don't know fully or at all, <u>feel free to take a break</u> and google it or follow my YouTube footsteps. The internet is the most powerful tool we have at our disposal, and the greatest repository of knowledge since the Great Library of Alexandria. Additionally, I encourage you to stop reading every half hour or hour and stand up to stretch and take a bathroom break, make or take a phone call or do something you have been putting off and listen to the thing I just referenced while you perform that dreadful task. Make sure to reward yourself with a snack and a <u>glass of water</u>. None of this is an easy read if you are HEALTHY let alone in pain and despair.*

The books in my home library, that I have amassed over my life, vary from a 1950's "First-year Latin" to Dungeons & Dragons 3.5 and 5th Edition sets of books as well as GURPS and the Saga Edition Star Wars Role-Playing Game. I have "Living with the

Taliban" next to "Raiders and Rebels: A Treatise on the Golden Age of Piracy", the "Norse Book of Runes" and Shel Silverstein's "Where the Sidewalk Ends" stacked on top for easy reference. "Beowulf" and the "Divine Comedy" are on the far sides but the "Book of Sith" and my well-worn "The Jedi Path" are side by side in the center near "The Art of War". "The Examined Life" (excerpts from Western Philosophers like Plato and Kant) and "The Story of Thought" (Greek Philosophers) have long been in my library. Tucked under the shorter books are my "Common Skills Handbooks" from the service.

"It is better to draw your water from many wells rather than just one; If a well goes dry or foul, you have other options." If you don't have options, maybe consider moving to a different mindset/routine/physical location/relationship dynamic/etc. for your personal health. The many sources concept is also true with sources of knowledge and styles or fields of learning. People always speak about looking at all sides of a situation and taking in other perspectives as a path to personal growth. I travelled the world literarily and learned from Western and Eastern philosophers, seeking an answer. <u>Much of this trail of study and thought is taught in college, but also easily accessible online or in wisdom shared via You-Tube videos.</u>

All of this travel led me to one place: Cynicism. I am a Cynic. The Classic Greek Philosopher, Diogenes is actually the first one my son mentioned to me. Cynics don't sugarcoat things. They see things for how they are (from THEIR perspective). I could choose to be a Stoic Cynic and accept things as they are, but I believe that in most cases this is the worse option. Another option is Absurdism: "the tried-and-true methods haven't worked… let's throw ideas against the wall until one sticks!" Now, I understand the classic Diogenes Laërtius. I am an Absurd Cynic like he was.

In my introduction, you see that there has been one constant in my life: loss and then gain. I was a damaged empath and so emotionally blinded, have been the victim of several narcissistic relationships that cost me everything each time it came to a close with my dismissal. I was repeatedly able to rebuild because in every loss, I had the opportunity to wallow or to change something. The gain comes when I act to change something I didn't like into something that I do like. I failed repeatedly in my path and only succeeded in dropping to a Dark Empath to protect myself, but also learned to hurt others with their own poison. Whenever I wallow in misery or feel I'm being taken advantage of, I become biting and dramatic to those around me on the rare occasion I'm not being reclusive. I had to learn through study, I had to answer that pained "WHY?" When I found the answer, I became a "Super Empath." (Google terms)

This has been a journey that almost destroyed me, but I kept pushing forward. **This is the first lesson: When you fall, look at why you fell and then get up and decide on a different way of doing things**. Doing the same actions in the same scenario that has already failed and still expecting success is the definition of insanity. The important part of this process is getting up. You could choose a different activity, or you could choose a different way to perform the action that failed after reviewing WHY it failed.

2022 was hard on me because I was in a period of self-destruction/self-discovery and stagnation or growth as a result. At the end of that year, I began to understand why I experienced everything. It's bizarre how much stuff falls into alignment the more you study. One of mine was Numerology. It listed 2022 as a Universal Year 6 for: love, healing, and relationships- I was blessed with a major relationship shift, but because I was negative the shift was negative.

Transpersonal Psychologist Abraham Maslow created the now famous Hierarchy of Needs (google this) which illustrates how human beings must first have their physiological needs met before finally reaching what he expressed as human actualization.

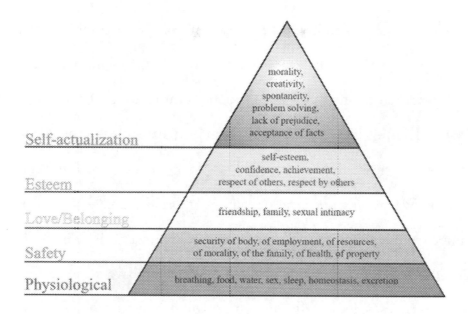

https://www.interaction-design.org

This is important because the sixth need presented in the Hierarchy of Needs' physiological section is homeostasis. Homeostasis is simply defined as; A state of balance among all the body systems needed for the body to survive and function correctly; calmness, smooth and even breathing, being hydrated and satiated in all needs. This also means not experiencing any of; anxiety, depression, excited-states, irritation, loneliness, maudlin or sad. This is easier said than done and is itself a constant process, but you are on the path.

The mantra that I keep repeating when people freak out over their being late (despite having overbearing punctuality trained into me) is; *"Time is a fictitious construct that man has created to assume some semblance of control over the chaos"*. As you will see later, mankind has used various calendars that vary widely. We then broke the day down into hours rather than simply morning, noon, afternoon, evening, and night. The person complaining might be confused, but if you think about it- time seems to drag in certain situations and fly in others. The more you look at a clock, the slower it seems to move. If you stop obsessing about the past (depression) or worrying about the future (anxiety), you can enjoy the present. The alternative is to anticipate the problem and take corrective measures. The military instilled in me a concept of "15 minutes prior", so that the senior man is never kept waiting on the junior man's arrival. This tactic became problematic when stacked in levels of command; the Platoon Commanding Officer issues the order that our Physical Training run starts at 0600 (6am in civilian-speak), the Platoon Sergeant says 0545, the section heads then pass on 0530 and expect you to be there at 0515 for the 0600 PT session. When only one layer deep it is a good idea and as a result I am almost never in a hurry (connecting flights cannot be helped, I prefer to drive instead if possible). This "fifteen minutes" allows flex time for long lights, bad drivers and traffic. If I notice that the fifteen minutes is not usually enough or I am driving through several large cities, I may add thirty minutes or more for a trip, dependent upon if I **need** to be punctual.

The mantra that I repeat when someone (including myself) complains about inefficient or feckless services or "house rules" that they encounter is "Not my circus, not my monkeys". This is to acknowledge that this is a "circus" to YOU, but it's okay because it is also **not your responsibility** to fix. When you understand that this problem is not yours unless you allow it to be in your life you will find peace. All you have to do is remove the circus from your influence (stop going there) and you will feel the relief. Find a new restaurant/bank/hotel/etc., and you may find another circus or you could discover something as good- if not better than you had before.

Another mantra that I repeat for things like the situation above and other events that impede my progress that I might be able to affect is one I got from Alcoholics Anonymous, the first part of the Serenity Prayer reads: "*God, grant me the serenity to <u>accept the things I cannot change</u>, courage to change the things I can, and the **wisdom to know the difference**.*" The rest of the prayer is more Taoist, but we will return to this concept. This part of the prayer will help you take even breaths between the commas and slow releases during the recitation to help you calm down before you make a mistake.

In each of the above situations, we are re-assessing and re-taking the power we had given away or mis-allocated. If you read the Hierarchy of needs from top to bottom, as some are wont to do, then I suggest you go back and read the levels from bottom to top. Reading the levels starting at the lowest basic needs, and then seeing those needs as they elevate rather than reduce to basic needs results in a different, and I think better psychological effect. You are starting to elevate your understanding.

At my darkest, I was a dangerous specter lashing out indiscriminately until satiated or banished. Despite all of this, no matter how many times my world was destroyed, I would reappear a few moments in time later with a new vigor, plumage, and direction.

I would like to think He would read this and laughingly say "whatever, kid", but I have taken the pen-name Diogenes the Phantom/Phoenix (Dio the Phoenix for my friends, which I offer to you-the reader). Honesty and love are required for growth. Delusion and hate are divisive and lead to your worst self.

> "Fear is the path to the dark side;
> Fear leads to anger, anger leads to hate,
> hate leads to suffering" -Jedi Master Yoda

One of my most prized possessions is a Greek bible that was printed in 1928. Etymology has long been a vice of mine, In English, words usually evolve from Greek or Latin roots but sometimes German and the Western world, as a whole, uses Arabic numerals. I have always thought that there was something missing from the Bible and thought it was simply lost in translation; It wasn't lost- it was removed.

Imperial Rome changed everything; the Calendar system, the Classic Greek Gods were renamed but largely remained very similar, and your options as a non-Roman in newly Roman conquered territory (your home and village) were to assimilate or die. If you need someone to pity in your darkest hours, think of those who have either been recently conquered or successfully repelled an invasion. Recent examples are; once Ukrainian Crimea, the Afghanistan Talib (or Learned Ones), Ukraine is in the process of repelling Russian fighters as I type this. The hell they have just endured is either going to worsen or lax due to their efforts.

While the religious authority of Imperial Rome was forcing, their new subjugates to speak their words and transcribing the histories, they had the power to change what they wanted. This implies intent over negligence which is what I prefer not to infer from behaviors of others, but in this case, there is sufficient evidence to suggest it. Much of this study involves languages I have not learned fully or have the drive to start (yet), but the internet connects us to others with similar ideas but different histories and proficiencies.

Latin is a fascinating language, but unique and frustrating because you operate with no articles (a, an, the). René Descartes wrote "Cogito Ergo Sum" and that translates to mean; I think (cogitate), therefore (wordsmiths still use ergo interchangeably), and I am (the sum of all my parts). This "I am" is highly relevant, and I will circle back to it later. Many of the languages that evolved from Latin have articles and various ways to alter language denoting gender- they wanted to be very clear.

It is possible to imagine the eager but overbearing Romans misinterpreting the idea of Christ or "Christos" as the Greeks said phonetically is spelled "Χρίστος" meaning anointed or sacred. The slight evolution etymologically to "Chrestos" is "Χρήστος" in Cyrillic originally meaning useful has also been used to represent ethical, righteous or just things. If you don't read or speak Greek or Russian derived languages then those words look almost identical and possibly sound the same.

A frustrated or impatient Roman could use them interchangeably to the dismay of their Greek instructor who may have even been a slave, as the only Citizens of Rome were born that way or granted citizenship by the people, generals, or emperors. It is at this point that I began to understand the divide between the Eastern Orthodoxy and the Entire

West. The ancient Hebrews were likely able to convey meaning into Greek, but when the Romans took everything- they literally re-wrote the book, thus masking the message.

I learned of an old book "God-Man: The Word Made Flesh" by George W. Carey on You-Tube that attempted to convey the results of research; the video is titled "104 yr Old Book reveals The Highest Secret Spiritual Knowledge" by "Motivation Manifested". Part 1 of the "God-Man" book starts;

> Primitive Christians, the Essenes, fully realized and taught the great truth that Christ was a substance, an oil or ointment contained especially in the Spinal Cord, consequently in all parts of the body as every nerve in the body is directly or indirectly connected with the wonderful "River that flows out of Eden (the upper Brain) to water the garden."
>
> The early Christians knew that the Scriptures, whether written in ancient Hebrew or Greek, were allegories, parables or fables based on the human body "fearfully and wonderfully made."

This "God-Man" book has several YouTube videos made with observations made by the video makers. If you haven't taken a break, I suggest one now.

Alan Watts gave a speech that, I accessed on YouTube, where he said that he believed that; "Jesus of Nazareth was a Human Being like [several other "prophets"] ...who early in life had realized a colossal experience of what we called cosmic consciousness." The problem with this cosmic consciousness is that the path to that doorway is through pain and growth. This is what I have slowly approached and rejected time and time again because I had emotional blocks and was loathe to do THAT work. Only recently did I perform the work needed and fully accept the "cosmic consciousness" after my latest experience. I am no prophet, I AM a son of a mortal man and woman, but I have studied these types of experiences and want to help you up out of your personal Hell- I have my map, let's see how yours compares.

Mr. Watts' speech is accessible through a "Dorothy Shelton" YouTube video titled, "The Real Message of Jesus." He suggests that "Christianity [has] institutionalized guilt as a virtue" by giving us an impossible example to follow in Jesus Christ. He mentions committing confession knowing that you ARE a sinner and will likely sin again, maybe not as intensely this time. The more you show contrition and penance the more devout or holy (whole-ly or complete) you should feel. I would like to offer a patch-fix for this and suggest <u>humility and altruism over any guilt</u> you may have. Whatever you did, you did in ignorance or fear. If the authorities feel the need to punish you, then accept your punishment to appease the local populace with the fulfillment of the laws in effect. He references John 10:30 KJV, where Jesus says "I and the Father are one" and the non-disciples around him gather stones to throw at him for blasphemy. Jesus then said, "Is it not written in your law, I have said "You are Gods", quoting the 82nd Psalm, "...because I have said I am *the* Son of God." Mr. Watts states that those italics refer not to emphasis but interpretation by the transla-tors. From the Greek bible, He states, it translates to "<u>A Son</u> of God", and this is the key problem to our understanding- **We are ALL sons and daughters of God. This is <u>your Second Lesson!</u> The core belief: love and protection**, not guilt and penance. This discovery is the "good news" that everyone preaches yet only grasps or offers partly or incorrectly. Go back and read it again! <u>God is everywhere including in each of us, We (this part means You SPECIFICALLY) are ALL a part of the greater God (**Community**), AND a God unto ourselves.</u> This is ONE CONCEPT- indivisible. This is how Jesus was both "a Son of God" as a "Begotten" being and a God Himself.

Some of us come from broken homes, single mothers or fathers due to neglectful or downright abusive parenting and it's extremely difficult to buy into the "Love and Protection" I'm attempting to preach. For your potentially horrific experiences, and those I have personally imparted on my family and community- I am truly sorry. Please take this in place of the apology that you likely never received; I choose to believe that your abuser was not able to comprehend that they were hurting you or even why they did it. I believe that every adult person is walking around with trauma, either resolved or unresolved. Some of this trauma the brain makes us forget "for our own safety," but the damage remains whether we recall it or not. The problem is that behavior learned in childhood shapes our behavior as an adult. Children learn; displays of affection, forgiveness, communication, physical and emotional distancing, respect/support, trust, and sharing/teamwork, from their parents and other adults. The abuse may have not even come from your parents but from a stranger or a family friend. Despite the source, if you were abused as a child, you may have refused to allow the same trauma, or after succumbing to your lowest self- fearing that you are becoming the abuser. The important aspect of this is that you recognize that the abuser was also damaged, and that your anger at them is not healthy. Therapy is a valuable tool for repairing the damage done, and this lesson of "love and protection" may lead you to forgive your abuser, and be able to protect the children in your family from similar trauma. If you are the abuser seeking forgiveness, you first need to forgive yourself. This act of (self)forgiveness can be difficult, but it is necessary for your emotional growth. If you do not forgive, you will dwell in misery or anger.

When You are downtrodden, it hurts us all because you may have destructive actions with others or yourself. When we are healthy, the self will understand that acceptance after failure is INEVITABLE, but so is getting up- how long you lay in the dirt is up to YOU. The country song "Love Without End, Amen" says it best- no matter what atrocity you commit- the Holy Father (and community as a whole) loves and accepts you. This is a harder thing to DO, let alone accept without guilt- but that's our part. "Vision boards" have been rising in popularity recently; the idea is you put together a board of what you want most in life and whatever you imagine will manifest. If this goal is foremost in your mind (like collecting and collaging pictures of what you want), then your mind is more focused on it and you may think of solutions you did not see before. The important part is to forgive yourself for falling- each time.

Remember that failure is necessary, not something to be avoided at all costs. If you never try, you won't fail but you will NEVER succeed. Healthy parents will usually give their offspring forgiveness if contrition is offered and it appears learning has occurred. If a crisis fills you with dread, then you are only seeing the negative, because a crisis is typically a time for growth. Yamabushido (@tsgbunting) posted on Facebook that;

> The word for "crisis" in Japanese, 危機 (Kiki) is written with the [characters that represent] "danger" and "opportunity". In other words, a crisis can be seen as a dangerous time, but equally as a time for opportunity. We have a choice over which one we see."

The imagery is clear; within each crisis is either the chance for danger or the opportunity for something different. When you accept that idea, you may feel less anxious and fearful.

After Mr. Watts spoke, a voice calling itself Yeshua spoke. Yeshua or Y'shua (ישוע; with vowel pointing <u>Hebrew</u>: יֵשׁוּעַ) was a common alternative form of that name. Yehoshua (<u>Hebrew</u>: יְהוֹשֻׁעַ), would become romanized into: *Yəhōšūaʿ*, 'Joshua' in later books of the <u>Hebrew Bible</u> and among Jews of the <u>Second Temple period</u>. Presented below are my calligraphic attempts of a few words in Hebrew and English (based on the calligraphy at "jewishvoice.org" that includes Aramaic).

ישוע Yeshua
ישועה Salvation
יהורה Judea
יהודי Jewish
ישראל Israel

The name Yeshua corresponds to the Greek spelling *Iesous* (Ἰησοῦς), then through the Latin *IESVS/Iesus*, comes the English spelling <u>Jesus</u>. This Y'shua said they do not like the name Jesus because of what it has come to represent. I wholly understand the sentiment, but He claims to restate his message and I encourage you to listen.

The council of Nicaea (now known as Iznik, Turkey) took place in 325 AD [anno (year of) domini (Lord)] and was assembled at the order of Roman Emperor Constantine I. This council of Christian Bishops from all across Christendom came to debate many things; to settle the divine nature of God the Son and His relationship to God the Father, the construction of the first part of the Nicene Creed, mandating the date of Easter, and promulgating early Cannon Law-deciding what books and testaments should be taught to all Christians. The "Arian Controversy" mainly debated whether or not being; born, created, and begotten, were the same or distinct. Here is the source of my problem with the way we see "I AM". The Oxford English Dictionary's second definition of "beget" is; give rise to; bring about. The example given is "success begets success" but I would debate that to enlighten or help ascend would be a good reason they would choose to say; "begotten, not made". It could have been a concession or appeasement of those believing that the Son was only Begotten (ascended) AFTER he was made (or born) and created (raised by his community). It was simply "lost in the shuffle"-one of my trigger phrases.

The council of Nicaea was held in 325 AD and the Library of Alexandria in Egypt dwindled during the Roman Empire from a lack of funding and support. Its membership appears to have ceased by the 260s AD. Between 270 and 275 AD, the city of Alexandria was invaded and retaken by the Empire in a counterattack that likely destroyed whatever remained of the Great Library, if it still existed at that time. The daughter library in the Serapeum may have survived after the main Library's destruction. The Serapeum was vandalized and demolished in 391 AD under a decree issued by the Coptic Christian Pope Theophilius of Alexandria but it does not seem to have housed books at the time and was mainly used afterwards as a gathering place for Neoplatonist philosophers.

Setting the date for Easter was the next issue before the council because for the early Christians, the observance of Easter coincided with the Jewish Passover and Feast of Unleavened Bread. Some early Christians had come to rely upon the Jewish locals for the date but had subsequently come to believe that the Jewish calendar was inaccurate. Catholicism wouldn't "correct" the Roman Julian Calendar until over a millennia later. The early Roman Church was assuming control of the religious narrative and has never let go.

I have used the Julian Calendar system for maintenance tracking (Consul Julius Caesar in 46 BC "reformed" the Roman calendar of 10 months that corresponded to signs in nature and launched the Empire from a small series of cities into something closer to what we commonly use today) and the Gregorian Calendar (Pope Gregory VIII modified the Julian Calendar in 1582 to correct the math error with a Leap Year added). If you look at the months in them both, there are traces of the old 10-month calendar; September was the seventh month, October the eighth, November the Ninth and December the tenth. The old Roman calendar started on what we know as the Spring Equinox in March.

There are numerous tomes in the Vatican possession to which they don't usually allow access. Mauro Biglino actually HAS had access to almost two dozen Vatican books by the request of the Vatican for translation. The YouTube channel "Vlad Racovita" goes into depth with his translations with the hope that more people look into them. The title of the video is "The Bible does not talk about God," and Mauro Biglino believes that we are descendants of star peoples. I voraciously read about aliens, as a pre-teen, to the point I had a nightmare that I was visited by "greys." I asked for a solution and the answer I was given was to stop thinking about it. I did, and had no further nightmares.

Part II of the same "God-Man" book starts: "There is no name under Heaven whereby ye may be saved except <u>Jesus Christed</u> and then crucified. (An alternative rendering of the Greek text, from Motivation Manifested video)". I take that new interpretation to mean that I should seek SALVATION (Y'shua or יְשׁוּעַת) for my past sins and anoint (mashach or וּמִלֵּאתָ) the world with my oil (Christ)- my gifts, and to be of service. This whole process began when I was praying and told God that I am his humble servant, his vessel. In this process, I realized that If I am persecuted, I should not resist- I am to remain humble and supplicate, as Jesus did and I am naturally hesitant to follow.

This is incredibly hard for me because I enlisted to become powerful and fearless. Now I have to be humble and meek? "Only the meek shall inherit the earth." Jordan Peterson has come out and stated THIS mistranslation. He said the closer meaning of the word for meek is "those with swords and knowledge but the understanding to keep them sheathed, shall inherit the earth." This is the basis for his whole "become dangerous" speeches, often misunderstood. In martial arts, one of the basic tenets is that the purpose of this training is self-defense only. You are training so hard to sharpen a skill that you hopefully never need to use. This is a similar sentiment shared by Veterans- We have skills that we hope to never have to use because once that monster is out it's hard to corral back into the pen. You have to accept your "crucifixion" or punishment when it comes because your sacred oil was spent in an unhealthy way or in the wrong place.

Jesus attracted too much attention, first as King of the Jews, then as a Healer and Sage, always mobile. Actively fighting a mobile insurgency is extremely difficult as we saw in Vietnam, Iraq and Afghanistan. The lessons keep repeating, you just need to listen and study so you pass the test that IS life. This message keeps being re-discovered and new religions founded on them. The Jewish Faith has held strong as the original wording remains and is rooted in their culture. Christianity has been translated and mistranslated repeatedly. Islam is so widespread like Christianity that it too has fractured and some cells are fanatical-choosing which parts of scripture to emphasize. I believe that Mormons have the right idea- but are lambs among the wolves. Many Eastern religions have a strong grasp on what I will present, but I think that Sikhism is the closest to what I now endear-especially with their "langar" communal feeding aspect.

If you watched the "God-Book" video I referenced earlier, you will recall that it describes a force that flows from your pineal gland down the spine. If it isn't spent or wasted in selfish acts, it will somehow change form and then flow back upward and reside in your solar plexus. "It charges itself there" for two and a half days, and on the moon cycle that correlates to your sun sign (Astrologic Sign) returns it to your pineal gland. It takes your energy- the way you are living and manifests it.

I have felt this many times but misunderstood it. Many people feel ulcers, migraines, or anxiety, then pop a pill to settle their stomach or some other "quick-fix" for any indication of a problem. The human body will tell you what is wrong, you just have to interpret what it is saying. Eastern practices like acupressure and beyond have entire posters and classes to manage these symptoms of ailments. I will not present it here, as I do not understand it fully and as partial or incorrect knowledge of this specific subject and others can be DANGEROUS. This is why I encourage you to do your own research. Ignoring these symptoms from your body is akin to putting tape over the check engine light in your car or playing music loud so you can't hear the engine noises. This manifestation is then taken up by the branches of the Pneumogastric Nerve and becomes the Fruit of "The Tree of Life" or the "Tree of Good and Evil." This is the part that hit home for ME; From the video, I inferred that "Good" means that you have behaved in balance and positivity with yourself and those around you and then your manifestation returns to the pineal gland to strengthen it and give you stronger Force. I then take "Evil" to mean the energy was wasted or spent in selfish or destructive ways, this causes ferment; acid and even alcohol, in the intestinal tract- thus the quote; "No drunkard can inherit the Kingdom of Heaven." The "God-Man" book states that "acids and alcohol cut, or chemically split the oil that unites with the mineral salts in the body and thus produces the monthly seed." When I read that passage, I understood why many religions eschew alcohol (Mormonism, Islam, etc.) and decided to follow that path. This will be hard as alcohol has long been my crutch, but has to also extend to other drugs, theft, promiscuity/ masturbation, fighting not in self-defense, or any other dishonor to myself or those around me. There is some evidence that ayahuasca, DMT and other psychotropic drugs bring people to "see God" and realize a greater "consciousness", but the problem with drugs is that the feeling can be addictive to the point of ruining your life chasing that first high. I have a very addictive personality, so this path is dangerous. That decision and many more like it are why I say I am a Grey Jedi; I work so hard to stay on the positive side, but can harness the negative. I understand that you (the reader) may be loath to stop drinking, but I imagine I will have a glass of wine with a meal every now and then- but only one. If my oil is copious and is only lightly thinned, it may be sufficiently viscous.

This sacred oil sounds a lot like the flow of "Chi" from Eastern religions and the Force in Star Wars. We have all been speaking in and watching parables. This message has been here all along, we just need to NEED a solution and become helpless (thanks Bill). I have needed a solution many times in my life and found myself powerless. After each time I got up, thought I understood, and pushed on. Christianity/Military Service/Fatherhood

were not the whole answer for me. Religion and family worked for my father, but as I will

reiterate- we are all different, with different learning styles.

		Represents	Balanced	Out of Balance	To Attain Balance	Healing Crystals
Western Name	Crown Chakra	Enlightenment, Unity, Infinity, Transcendence, Source	Connected to Higher Self/Source, Trust in the Universe, Being present and concious	Detached from Source, Strict Religious Views, Closed-minded, Depressed, Confused	Declare your highest intentions, Release what no longer serves you, Spend time in meditation and prayer, Find stillness and silence	Amethyst, Lepidolite, Charoite, Selenite, Clear Quartz, Howlite, Rainbow Moonstone
Eastern Name	Sahasrara					
Associated Color(s)	Violet/White					
Location	Top of Head					
Western Name	Third Eye	Intuition, Dreams, Spirituality, Psychic Abilities, Vision/Wisdom, Imagination	Intuitive, Spiritual, Self aware, Imaginative, Open-minded, Focused, Clear Thoughts/Vision	Nightmares, Forgetful, Anxiety, Lack of Inner Guidance, Low Self awareness, Headaches	Practice visualization, Spend time abosrbing sunlight, yoga, journal, stargaze	Amethyst, Lapis Lazuli, Iolite, Fluorite, Tanzanite, Auralite 23, Sodalite, Labradorite
Eastern Name	Ajna					
Associated Color(s)	Indigo					
Location	Between Eyebrows					
Western Name	Throat Chakra	Communication, Truth, Expression, Speaking, Listening, Independence	Healthy Boundaries, Clear Communication, Active Listener, Speak your Truth	Fear of Speaking Up, Over-talking, Lying, Lack of Boundaries, Argumentative	Chant, sing or write, Explore your inner child, Drink soup with warming spices	Aquamarine, Apatite, Amazonite, Larimar, Sodalite, Angelite, Kyanite, Turquoise
Eastern Name	Vishuddha					
Associated Color(s)	Blue					
Location	Throat					
Western Name	Heart Chakra	Love & Compassion, Relationships, Trust, Forgiveness, Healing, Respect, Gratitude	Empathetic, Grateful, Ability to Give and Receive Love, Compassionate, Kind, Trustworthy	Jealous, Cold-hearted, Selfish, Unempathetic, Victim Mindset, Co-dependent	Reach out to a friend, Forgive someone, Spend time in nature where the air is fresh, eat fresh green vegetables	Malachite, Emerald, Rose Quartz, Ruby, Rhodochrosite, Green Aventurine, Rhodonite
Eastern Name	Anahata					
Associated Color(s)	Green/Pink					
Location	Center of Chest					
Western Name	Solar Plexus	Self-worth, Identity, Willpower, Ego, Goals, Success, Empowerment	Confident, Assertive, Manifestation, Active, Optimistic, Reliable, High-Self-esteem	Poor Self-image, Extra Critical, Worthlessness, Egotistical, Passive, Greedy, Poor Digestion	Spend time near fire, Eat fermented foods, ginger and turmeric root	Citrine, Pyrite, Golden Tiger Eye, Amber, Honey Calcite, Golden Healer Quartz
Eastern Name	Manipura					
Associated Color(s)	Yellow					
Location	2" Above Navel					
Western Name	Sacral Chakra	Pleasure, Creativity, Emotions, Physical, Energy, Sexuality, Reproduction	Motivated, Emotional Intelligence, Flowing Creativity, Energetic, Balanced Sex Drive	Sexual Dysfunction, Addiction, Lethargy, Fear of Emotional & Sexual Intimacy, Guilt	Spend time near water, Get out of your comfort zone, Explore creative hobbies, Socialize and connect with people	Carnelian, Tangerine Quartz, Orange Calcite, Sunstone, Copper, Peach Moonstone
Eastern Name	Svadhisthana					
Associated Color(s)	Orange					
Location	Pelvis					
Western Name	Root Chakra	Grounding, Security, Safety, Survival, Instincts, Stability, Kundalini	Grounded, Basic Needs Met, Sense of Security, Stability & Regularity	Fearful, Unstable Life Circumstances, Low Energy, Sense of Lack, Anxiety, Ungrounded	Do some gardening, Spend some time in dirt, Sit under a tree and feel the earth beneath, Eat root vegetables	Garnet, Red Jasper, Hematite, Bloodstone, Red Tiger Eye, Ruby, Black Tourmaline
Eastern Name	Muladhara					
Associated Color(s)	Red					
Location	Base of Spine					

Western nationalities typically aren't as exposed to the Chakras or the concept of

a "Third Eye", but Eastern philosophy and religion are central in our path. This chart

was created referencing several sources, but is clearly represented on the website bud-

dhismguide.com. You may notice that the colors of the lower 5 chakra presented there

align with the needs chart on page 5. This is because this is our lowest self and the same

as any other animal in creation- they all voice, pump fluids, are aware of others, digest

and excrete as well as reproduce (Root, Sacral, and Solar Plexus Chakra). The difference in Humanity is that we possess the Third Eye Chakra and Crown Chakra but they may not be accessible or open. Physical Exercise, Karate, Yoga or Tai-Chi are good ways to open the flow of energy or sense where the problems lay. A professional massage tends to help knotted muscles and blocked chakras.

The Yin-Yang is addressed in Chapter Seven and the Triple Comet design that I pulled from Japanese design is covered in Chapter Nine. This art has become mainstream but they are symbolic of a greater knowledge. I own a single singing bell as that is all I desire, there are (seed or bija mantra) chants for each of the chakras. Most of us recognize the "Om" (ॐ) as the prime symbol and mantra from Hinduism, but it is said to be the sound of creation and of the universe. I have several prayer bracelets and have had catholic rosaries and nice watches. All I wear is my dog-tags from the service-electrical taped so they don't make noise but are still present in case of car accident. My phone tells me the time, date, and weather. I usually am barefoot and in plain clothes. I have become a minimalist as have many others on this path.

There is one video on You-Tube that I actually ask you to watch; the channel "Quazi Johir" posted the video "1200 yr Old Sacred Text Reveals How To Bend Reality With Mind". The reason I request this is three-fold; 1) "Quazi" states that He has spent 7 years devoting his life to this practice, 2) His walk-through of the breathing exercise is excellent and I suggest that you practice it, and 3) The suggestions "Quazi" presents are good guidelines on your path.

I encourage (not ask or demand) each of you readers to limit your purchases to ONE of each thing that You think that You need (houses, cars, boats, etc.) and only purchase another if the needs change, the needs aren't met, or the implement is irreparable. Too often we throw money at more quantity of what made us happy when we attained one singly; cars, guns, houses, relationships, millions of dollars, etc.). Diogenes the Dog lived in a used barrel and ate what food was available for as little cost as possible, and He CHOSE that life. This is the message of minimalism, less clutter leaves less to maintain, less to clean and move. I am constantly downsizing my things, but the books and my art will never leave me. My next aspiration is to learn guitar- but that takes devotion. I already own a single guitar (Fender acoustic) and when ready, I will return to my lessons as I haven't fingered chords in years.

There is a story/parable/metaphor where one soldier is walking by and sees a friend in a deep pit (depression) and where so many others had said they would go get help but they never returned, or the help was not sufficient. This time the soldier jumped into the pit with him and the soldier at the bottom screamed; "What are you doing? Are you nuts? Now you're stuck here too!" The other soldier replied, "It's okay, Brother- I've been here before, let me show you the way up."

The knowledge and references in this book are "the way up". I have made an emotional climbing kit of everything that works for me. I know myself more than any other person. When you use this book, you have to approach with an open mind and humility- you don't know everything. It's okay, neither do I but I am doing my best and constantly revising each chapter as I personally grow more. Some of this may confuse you- ask for clarification from friends and family. If you have access to the internet, then I encourage you to Google and YouTube everything in this book.

Notes:

_____

_____

_____

_____

_____

_____

_____

_____

_____

Congratulations! That was a long journey that was only the highlights and epiphanies of my studies. Take a break or google some of what I presented

You can skip the next two chapters if you like. I only introduce the "Love Cards" Astrological system in Ch II. The MBTI (Ch III) is a personality typing system that is extremely thorough and I believe the source of many Pantheons

CHAPTER II

LOVE CARDS [1997]

WHEN CONTRACTING ON THE ISLAND of Oahu in Hawaii, I rented a room from a woman who taught me many things over the months I stayed- one of which was that I am a "9 of hearts" (Universal Love/Constant Disappointment) in a personality typing system she had learned. This system is called "Love Cards" by Robert Lee Camp and uses your birthdate to determine your cosmic gift and cosmic curse as well as so much more. Maggie said that in her life, she was excellent at finding faults in systems and coding. She's found fault in all of the other systems but this one speaks true to her. Let it be your introduction as it was to me on this difficult path, or you can skip it entirely- Your choice. I have presented pictures of some of the books released. The system is enlightening but far too large for me to regurgitate here, however it is an assignment with substantial return. I elect to not teach the love cards process here as it is not required for balance, however IT IS the reward/punishment for walking the tightrope. Let me expound:

Universal Love: I am a font of positive energy, but a well that can run dry or be soiled. I crave to help my friends and can easily project and detect emotions. If I don't control the flow of energy, I am prone to destruction from outside corruption or giving to the point that I'm drained. This has repeatedly happened. I was ignorant then but have grown emotionally and spiritually.

Constant Disappointment: I naturally look for and find problems to fix. I am overly critical of myself, others, and systems- this served me as a repairman, student, and instructor but is also the deep spiral I can throw myself into with dark thinking and rumination.

If you read the Love Cards books, it will help you understand that people still wonder why they do what they do as they have for eternity. In the back of the books, it even suggests likely relationship success and problems between the different cards. In this facet, I observed it to mimic the eastern or western zodiacs, more match making – but that's what all of these systems *could* be used for. The Enneagram creators were worried that if wisdom of the Enneagram became widespread, it would be reduced to a parlor game The MBTI (next chapter) is often referred to in dating scenes. I learned these systems to understand myself, not seeking a mate. I was so broken that I decided any girlfriend I had would either be a distraction from my personal growth or an anchor to a drowning man.

The first step in this personal growth for you is loving yourself- often the hardest step is to love the person who caused all these problems. How can anyone love you when you don't love yourself? Only when You love yourself can You actually want yourself to get better. The only person who can help you is YOU. Wanting to get better means taking actions like seeking help when you need but cannot perform. Wanting to get better means being honest with yourself as to why you are unhappy and how Your actions caused the events that made you unhappy. Therapists can ask you questions and guide your thinking but you have to do all the heavy emotional lifting yourself between sessions and yes, I have a therapist- SHES AMAZING! Every step of personal growth is through the veil of pain, accept this as the price.

"The journey of a thousand miles begins with a single step" -Lao Tzu

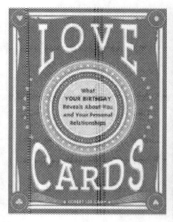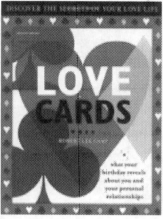

These books are reference material; If you want to know YOUR cosmic reward and punishments, you need to put in the effort.

I love you, and hope you do too.

CHAPTER III

MYERS-BRIGGS TYPE INDICATOR [1962]

THE PURPOSE OF THE MEYERS-BRIGGS Type Indicator (MBTI) personality inventory is to make the theory of psychological types described by Carl Jung accessible and useful in people's lives. In my quest to understand myself, some of the first research I did was to find my "personality type"; I am an INTJ. The tests ask you many questions about your preferences in a variety of situations. You could take the test (and pay for the results), but I recommend you just study the types and you will understand yours. It's been said that the MBTI is more than just a test, it's a process. "We don't say 'here are the results, good luck', we say 'here are the results, now let's talk that through to make the results more relevant to your reality' " (from mindbodygreen.com). I suggest that if you want to dig deeper than I present in this tome, you pursue your own course of study.

The letters for each psychological type refer to these four major factors;

- Favorite World: Outer (E for extroverted), or Inner (mental) (I for introverted)

- Information Management: Face Value (S for sensing), or Interpretation (N for intuition, I know it's weird, but they had already used I)

- Decision: Logic & Consistency (T for thinking), or the specific Situation and Circumstances (F for feeling)

- Structure: Decide & Stay True (J for judging), or stay flexible for new options (P for perceiving)

The ANALYSTS: "We are thinkers, not robots!"

Known for their rationality as they decide with their head, not heart.

They are driven to understand and create, find out for themselves.

They love ideas and speculation more than the realities of follow-through.

They are also relentless self-improvers (seeming to rise from the ashes).

They are socially selective and prone to brusque speech if pushed.

INTJ, The Architect: Imaginative and strategic thinkers maing a series of plans with contingencies for every event.

INTP, The Logician: Innovative inventors with an unquenchable thirst for knowledge and power.

ENTJ, The Commander: Bold, imaginative and strong-willed leaders who always find a way (or make one).

ENTP, The Debater: Smart, witty, and curious thinkers who cannot resist an intellectual challenge.

The DIPLOMATS: "Leap and the net will appear"

They seek to connect with others and often have powerful insight.

They are naturally optimists but can be triggered to self-righteousness.

They can be tempted to ignore mundane tasks for big dreams and ideas.

They have a big heart and will usually volunteer first for tasks.

They need to bring progress to the group, but still needs to belong.

INFJ, The Advocate: Quiet and mystical, yet very inspiring and tireless idealists.

INFP, The Mediator: Poetic, kind and altruistic people, always eager to help a good cause.

ENFJ: The Protagonist: Charismatic and inspiring leaders, able to mesmerize their listeners.

ENFP: The Campaigner: Enthusiastic, creative and sociable free spirits, can always find a reason to smile.

The SENTINELS: "If it works, don't break it"

They are naturally cooperative, practical and grounded.

They seek order, security, and stability- will work hard to maintain it!

They tend to be self-motivated and productive but expect that of others.

They offer stability and wisdom and are bolstered when it is returned.

They can be stubborn but loathe drama.

They show love more in actions than words or gifts.

ISTJ: The Logistician: Practical and fact-minded individuals whose reliability is infallible.

ISFJ: The Defender: Very dedicated and warm protectors, ever ready to defend their loved ones.

ESTJ: The Executive: Excellent administrators, unsurpassed at managing things, not people.

ESFJ: The Consul: Extraordinarily caring, social and popular people always eager to help.

The EXPLORERS: "What's Next?"

They tend to be self-reliant, quick thinkers and delight in those situations.

They tend not to be obsessed with precise details and appreciate a good idea today rather than the perfect idea tomorrow.

They tend to have open minds to new concepts but can be flighty if tied down.

They are exciting, innovative, and want to share their finds with others.

They are likely to avoid commitment, but if you can keep their attention you might be able to hold their heart.

ISTP: The Virtuoso: Bold and practical experimenters, masters at various tools.

ISFP: The Adventurer: Flexible and charming artists, ready to explore and experience something new

ESTP: The Entrepreneur: Smart, energetic and very perceptive people who truly enjoy living on the edge.

ESFP: The Entertainer: Spontaneous, energetic and enthusiastic people-life is never boring around them.

There are subsets of each personality type here also, personalitopia.com presents them in depth however I will not delve that deep. The subsets represent the varying levels of assertiveness, playfulness, seriousness, and turbulence in each MBTI Type. Should you want to know more, you can research it the way you desire. As an example, I will present my subsets;

- INTJ A+ "The Leader" possesses a strong will that they put into projects that they are passionate about while understanding that failure is an option.

- INFJ T- "The Follower" is very concerned with their fame, status or worth to the group and can be overly self-critical.

- INTJ A- "The Fighter" is a lone wolf or independent spirit who goes against societies norms and expectations but can be angry at society or themselves

- INFJ T+ "The Pleaser" wants to present a positive, cheerful and easy to like image to their world but they crave approval and appreciation.

I have at one time or another personified each of these naturally and can now more readily direct my flow from one to the next despite my level of turbulence and assertiveness using wisdom, which is really memories of what doesn't work.

This has been enlightening, but what comes next is more painful.

CHAPTER IV

THE ENNEAGRAM OR NINE-SIDED SHAPE

"No one intentionally does evil; they always choose an apparent good"

– Thomas Aquinas

THE ENNEAGRAM IS ANOTHER PERSONALITY typing system, but instead of looking at how you do things, it looks at WHY you do things- and now there are NINE types! That's not all- learning this system will HURT you emotionally because it has to do with our fatal flaw, our perpetual sin or downfall. You won't WANT to learn this part because it picks at the scars that brought you to this book- it is emotionally triggering, but this part is pivotal to understanding and attaining perspective.

"LIFE is pain, Highness. Anyone who says differently is selling something"

-The Dread Pirate Westley.

The "crux of the situation" is that to be at peace or in balance, you will have a <u>mental or emotional or physical boundary you will have to overcome</u>. When you do, its liberating, empowering, and comforting- you are the order in a whirlwind. This state is the nirvana we have been chasing, and you can then open your third eye (later chapters still).

I am by no means an expert on the Enneagram and will not explain every example situationally. I believe that wise King Solomon taught the "Demons" (unhealthy) their lessons through labors as education, and that Ancient Judaism listed Angels and Demons alongside their behaviors in an attempt to educate the masses as I am here. If you seek a further understanding of the Enneagram- seek that knowledge on your own. Understanding the Enneagram is PIVOTAL to maintaining balance- This is your "steering wheel"

Name (Intent)	Behaviors: positive or negative situationally

1 The Perfectionist (Reformer)
     Cosmic Gift: Serenity
     Cosmic Curse: Resentment
	Workaholic, absolutist, perfectionist, people pleaser, believes "I am good", anal-retentive, needs to be the best

2 The Giver (Helper)
     Cosmic Gift: Pride
     Cosmic Curse: Humility
	Presents their best/worst self, empathetic, when negative, can be extremely cruel, codependency, needs to be desired

3 The Performer (Motivator)
     Cosmic Gift: Integrity
     Cosmic Curse: Deceit
	Naturally intuit efficiency, conflicted, dynamic energy, more effective in a group, prefer to repress heart, needs success

4 The Romantic (Artist)
     Cosmic Gift: Equanimity
     Cosmic Curse: Envy
	Eccentric, dramatic, flamboyant, maudlin, moody, dark, tragic, destructive, needs to be special

Name (Intent)	Behaviors: positive or negative situationally
5 The Observer (Thinker)	Absent-minded prof., assimilates data,
Cosmic Gift: Detachment	loves books and libraries, very controlled,
Cosmic Curse: Avarice	don't want to be seen, needs free space
6 The Questioner (Loyalist)	Extremely loyal, conformist, anxiety prone,
Cosmic Gift: Courage	sees danger everywhere, safe in numbers
Cosmic Curse: Fear	scapegoater, needs an enemy to demonize
7 The Epicure (Generalist)	Most likeable of all types, most positive,
Cosmic Gift: Joy	eternal child, gourmand, prone to indulge,
Cosmic Curse: Gluttony	needs to fill a void
8 The Boss (Leader)	Most negative of all types, loves vulgarity,
Cosmic Gift: Zest for Life	appreciates oppositional energy or power,
Cosmic Curse: Passion	afraid of direct intimacy, need to boss
9 The Mediator (Peacemaker)	Appears lazy/no energy, huge self-image
Cosmic Gift: Focus	floats through life, easy to forget
Cosmic Curse: Sloth	procrastinator, needs structure

These types each have one of three sub-types: self-preservation, social and sexual (or one-to-one) that more specifically represent individuals within their type based upon drive. Dr. Tom LaHue and Fr. Richard Rohr are experts on the enneagram, please You-Tube your types and subtypes.

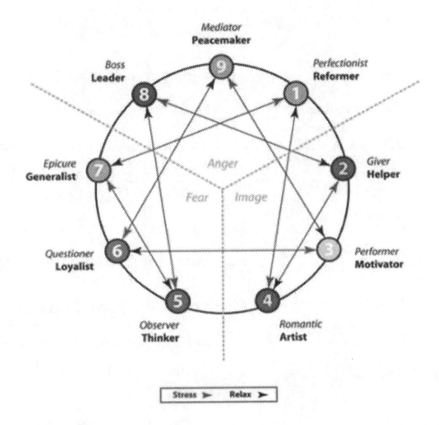

This diagram is also known as **"The Nine Faces of God."** (pulled from professional-leadershipinstitute.com) The nine major personality types fall into three areas:

> Body: These types typically learn by doing the action themselves.
>   Weakness: Anger
> Heart: These types usually learn by watching demonstrations.
>   Weakness: Image
> Head: These types typically learn by reading instructions Weakness: Fear

THE WINGS

Each of these personality types is influenced by and resentful of one wing each respectfully, meaning your personality will want to personify one of your "neighbor" numbers and resent the other "neighbor." I am a 5w6, meaning that I am the Observer that wants to belong. 6 is a fear type and my healthy response is a phobic 6- let the group decide what to do about problems because I want to belong. When I am unhealthy, I tend to exhibit the counterphobic 6 and take matters into my own claws. I also personify the negative aspects of 4 (the other, un-named neighbor): loves to roll in my own depression, dramatic and needs to be special (I took on the name of a classic philosopher!). As you can see, we embody both wings, whether desired or not.

One concept I have postulated is that we all have one Angel wing and one Demon wing- the little voices on your shoulders! More metaphors, but it makes sense; If we learn how to embody both wings in a positive aspect then we are Angelic, but if we use the habits and skills of both wings for selfish or negative actions then we seem Demonic. I have long believed that the Heaven we all seek is found in peace in the here and now, and we each make our own Hell in our selfish actions. Only now do I understand that they were right; whatever you imagine you will manifest. This part is a FACT: whatever you imagine, or pray for puts some energy out in the Universe and does something that even I don't understand. Put out positivity and get it back in a surprise, put out negativity and you get to see someone else's worst side. How do we use this?

THE UP WING

The positive aspects of this number are what you crave to do, they fill your well. For me, they are 3 (performer) and 6 (questioner) [Why two? Wait for Chapter Seven, finish this part first]. I truly delight in the accomplishment of fixing or improving something as well as improving myself. I've voraciously absorbed most of this information as a type 5 (observer) and have enjoyed my time as an instructor. The things in your up-wing bring you joy and produce more positive energy/fill Your spiritual well. When you are feeling down, do these actions to feel better. I paint, improve Magic: the Gathering decks, learn new things, or host a D&D game. This part comes easily.

What are Your healthy behaviors? _____

_____

How often do you make time to do them? _____

_____

THE DOWN WING

The negative aspects of this number are what you are naturally loathe to do, they drain your energy and corrupt what positivity you had. It is also what gets you in trouble. For me they are 1 (perfectionist) and 4 (romantic). I can re-work a sentence or alter the font until kingdom come, it will drive me batty and as for maudlin, brooding and dramatic, don't go there. The destructive part comes when something doesn't meet my expectation: slow/bad drivers, bad service at restaurants, being taken advantage of by someone I trusted, or simply having a crappy day- I get angry. I scream, I rage, I say mean spirited things and even swear at something/someone or take negative physical action. I just need to let you know how upset You made me, but for what purpose? So that You don't do it again, if they even care after my reaction- this doesn't work. Some people out there will simply do it again because you challenged them. This is why I kept looking for an answer; I know it is unacceptable behavior yet I perpetrate it on my family, friends and strangers.

What are your unhealthy behaviors? _____

_____

What do you keep doing that you wish to stop? _____

_____

Who have you hurt? _____

_____ ,Yourself

Healthy Shift

When we are healthy (whole) and sane, we naturally exhibit the positive aspects of another type. When a 5 is healthy, they act from the positive aspects of the 8 (the Boss) [This refers to the black arrow from 5 to 8 on page 37]. The knowledge we've amassed can be put to good use and when we exude positivity, we are of most service to each other. This is the ideal state of mind and is what I strive for in every situation, but it can be exceedingly difficult. It was in this mindset that I ran my simulators and my storefronts. My wives always asked why I always talk about how the military does it- because we learned the thought process to accomplish anything to be able to do the seemingly impossible. While in service, I was transferred from the repair section to being in charge of several issuing sections in series, each only long enough to inventory gear, induct items into maintenance and teach the issuing sections how their job was supposed to be done according to the manual. My commands each knew exactly how to put my skills to use long before I did. It is in this benevolent and loving mindset that I transcribe this knowledge and direction, I want us all to make healthy efforts and forge better lives. In so doing, I wish to atone for all of the evil I have done in ignorance.

Where does your number go when Healthy? _____

Unhealthy Shift

If our mind is not whole or sane (sanus meaning healthy in Latin, also insane means not healthy/whole), then we can get the message and not still understand the purpose. When a 5 is unhealthy, they act from the negative aspects of the 7 [The red arrow from 5 to 7 on page 32] (Epicure/Gourmand) by acting childish, indulging in vulgarity, drugs and alcohol, dangerous behavior, etc.- always trying to "fill the void". I used my skills for selfish

ends over altruism, often to the detriment of myself but sometimes others are involved.

Where does your number go when unhealthy? _____

This has been some of the hardest part of this trail, take a break, then review.

CHAPTER V

ENERGY/CHI/THE FORCE/ GOOD AND EVIL

HAVE LIVED MOST OF MY life unknowingly passing along the negative energy I absorbed and this has caused me life-devastating problems as I wrote earlier. You have to <u>do the work</u> to understand how to consciously change; to divert or modulate negative energy to positive energy.

Heart based numbers (2, 3, 4) usually learn how to this through social interaction in school, daycare, or with siblings. Body based numbers (8, 9, 1) usually learn this through work or instruction at formal schools. Head based numbers (5, 6, 7) tend to have to take psychology classes, philosophy classes, read a ton of books and take tons of tests. Because I was body damaged, I was stunted in that area and prone to anger. I learned in school and the service how to manage my reaction by either suppressing my emotions if they conflicted or by using the suppressed emotions to accentuate my reaction. They encouraged the Maudlin Perfectionist. I was trained how to unhealthily modulate, but didn't understand that it was actually unhealthy. I kept having the same angry and passionate problems, nothing improved. I did not understand what I learned and applied, so I could not reliably predict what would work. Imagine learning the slope and intercept of a line (y=mx+b), but not knowing how to graph the line or find the x-intercept. Another way to say that would be to say I had an emotional blockage. Some of my readers already understand some of the content of this book, others may understand less. I would be pleasantly surprised if you already understood all of the contents of this book from a different perspective, and I tip my figurative cap to you- Sempai or Rabbi.

Returning to my Jedi/Sith analogy to this all, in my mind- the Force (energy) is like electricity. It is all around us, it fires synapses in our brain, it allows us to move muscles while operating the laptop I type this on and power the internet that I pull my sources from. It can be used for immense good, but also acts of evil- intent is everything. Electrical energy and its fields tie us all together and unite us. The human body is itself a chemical power plant (the Matrix knew this). Food goes in, the stomach acid breaks it down and the intestines absorb nutrients. This is used to generate energy and is then either used for kinetic motion (walking, lifting, playing) or stored long term in fat cells.

If you eat a lot of carbohydrates and fats on top of the protein you need to survive and aren't very active, then your fat cells store more energy for later- this is how we are designed. If you have a diet rich in starches and proteins but stay active constantly then the carbohydrates go into the movement and the protein repairs the muscle fibers that tear. These fibers get bigger but also produce lactic acid that sits in the muscles (chemical waste) and if you then drink water and either massage the area yourself or pay for a massage, the lactic acid is pushed back into your circulation and comes out as urine. If you are already overweight and only eat fatty foods and proteins and ZERO carbohydrates and maintain a moderate lifestyle (think Atkins diet) then you are pooping out most of the fat as the body doesn't need to use energy to break it down to make more of what it already has. You will lose weight; however, you will drive your body to ketosis which is hard on the kidneys and liver. You need to drink water constantly to flush your system of all the chemical waste resulting from breaking down fat.

When you take alcohol, drugs, or pharmaceuticals, trace amounts of stuff are left in fat and enters your circulation when the energy is broken down for use-possibly to cool your body as sweat. I have succeeded in weight loss on the Atkins or No-Carb diet. If you are on this type of program, when you return to your old way of eating- it all comes back. You have to instead enter phase 2 of the Atkins program and slowly step in carbohydrates back into your system- I prefer carrots and other veggies as they are forbidden in phase one but also contain a lot of water and fiber- needed to flush your system. When you get to the point you are no longer losing weight each day- that is your equilibrium for the amount of activity you performed. IF you want to keep eating more carbs, you will need to step up the physical activities. If you want more weight loss, stay where you are and be more active. If you don't want to be more active, then go back to Phase 1. In this way you are giving your body the reminder that carbs are out there, then we start burning fat again. If you never leave Phase 1, I have observed that you stay in ketosis despite drinking lots of water and stop losing weight after a few months. It seems to me that you suffer without any gains. In whatever diet, the protein keeps you alive and the body generates energy.

CHAPTER VI

RESONANCE OR FREQUENCY

I MAGINE A SINE WAVE, THIS represents the Alternating Current (AC) that is generated from hydroelectric dams or wind energy or the alternator in cars. Now, imagine that instead of taking the peaks and troughs, you only wanted the peaks. For that you would need a full wave rectifier to make the negative wing of that sine wave into another positive wing. The problem now is the troughs are at Zero instead of -240V or whatever.

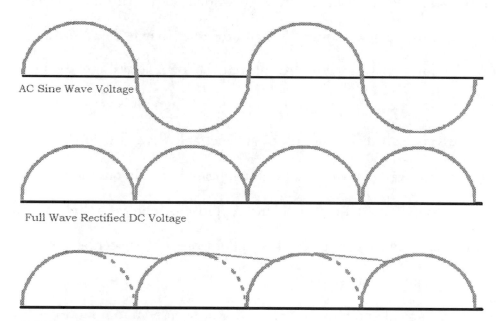

AC Sine Wave Voltage

Full Wave Rectified DC Voltage

Full Wave Rectified Voltage with Filtering

Now we know that we need a power converter. The difference is that the power converter is taking that set of positive arches of voltage and then adding a capacitive circuit to turn those troughs into ripples. There are some tertiary filtering circuits to smooth those ripples so that the drop in voltage is not noticeable and you get a more consistent Direct Current energy output. Instead of powering your laptop or game system, this energy powers your heart, your brain and interacts with every other living being as if it was an open Wi-Fi connection. Until you understand how to block, channel and convert the negative energy that life throws at you- you will always be fearful.

My Son and I loved the Nickelodeon "Avatar: The Last Airbender" animated series. In it there are four major nations: Fire (Speech), Water (Empathy), Earth (Body), and Air (Spirit). The series begins with the fact that the Avatar, who can master all four "bending (element modulating)" styles, has disappeared. The introduction to the show is that the Fire Nation has already destroyed the Air Nation (Knowledge with passionate rage has killed spirit metaphorically). We found out in season one that the Southern Water Tribe has had all of their known benders taken and that the Northern Water Tribe is the last redoubt of this skill. We find out they have the Moon Spirit (Tui) in a hidden pool. Tui has a counterpart in the pool named "La" and together they form a Yin-Yang. The spiritual knowledge for empathy is still present, but the lower levels of empathy have been incapacitated by more passionate speech. The Earth Kingdom is largely commoners but there is a fortress city called Ba-Sing-Se or "Impenetrable City." The Fire Nation is almost able to penetrate the wall, but then the Avatar appeared. It's a good watch, the live action movie that came out soon after took a different approach. There is an earth bending based Avatar series being produced after "The Legend of Korra" (the water bender based Avatar sequel to the animated Avatar series).

As an interesting side-note to this, there is a near-perpetual motion machine at the

Royal Society in London, England. Adam Savage did a few episodes of "Tested" on it and I saw it in YouTube (yep, again). I believe that I now know how it works (watch the video on it first). There are three electromagnetic power generators 120 degrees out of phase with wound copper wire around the U-shaped stationary frames, the rotating circle has three boxes that pass through- that I think are filled with a magnetized rare earth metal. I think that they then input three sine waves 120 degrees out of phase through independent full wave rectifiers and trickle filters. I am hypothesizing that they then combine the DC voltage in series to add together for the next step: the box in the center of the frame serves to create an electric field around the two pins near the bearings that serve to push and pull on the metallic cups on the rotating wheel and induce a new "push and pull" force with the electricity created by the motion it already had. Does this sound familiar? The bearings are probably primed with graphite, as oil or grease tends to gum-up over time. All the machine would need is a push every few years (decades?) to overcome the slow reduction in energy that, although minimized, is inescapable. They probably recharge the graphite and replace the magnetic source and then, just give it a push. I don't think the device has the ability to store energy like we do.

In sports both directly competitive (tennis, baseball, basketball) and self-reflective (golf, darts, swimming) there are known times when the skill you demonstrated is not available. It may be called the "Yips", the 'Shanks" or simply "not in the zone" where you just feel "off." The events in your mind, emotional and psychological, take you out of "the groove." These are all times of imbalance that affect your body. Some athletes adhere to a certain diet or ritual to maintain that balance- not truly understanding WHY it works, just that it does have results. The problem usually goes away "with time" or the problem player goes away. They are forced to deal with the imbalance or it destroys the athlete. When you pull a muscle, you take it easy; massage the area, take medicine, and allow it time to heal. The same can be done with emotional (spiritual) and psychological (mental) damage. You have to be psychologically and emotionally present to recognize the damage and decide to love yourself enough to make time for you to address the issue and resolve it. Resolution is rarely easy nor quick, but necessary for maintaining balance and staying "in the groove" you have established. If your groove is set at too low a level, make a new groove,

How do we do this for ourselves? When you're feeling degraded-go to your safe place and recharge, take a shower or bath, dress up for just you or get into comfy clothing (whatever makes YOU happy). You are cleaning the "outside of your temple", now you need to clean the inside. Trash the pizza boxes of success parties, wash the dishes of past relationships, and take out the garbage of past failures- the time for rumination is over. Doing this periodically cleans the "room" in the temple that you live in- your mind. Less clutter around means less to trip over (trigger) in everyday conversation. When you feel ready; give yourself a little push and get out there, be observant of the energy around you, what you take in and give out, be present.

Map of Conciousness (Black and White Interpretation)

Built upon the ideas Developed by David R. Hawkins

	Name of Level	Energetic Log	Predominant Emotional State	View of Life	God-View	Process
Spiritual Paradigm	Enlightenment	700-1000	Ineffable	Is	Self	Pure Conciousness
	Peace	600	Bliss	Perfect	All-Being	Illumination
	Joy	540	Serenity	Complete	One	Transfiguration
	Love	500	Reverence	Benign	Loving	Revelation
Reason & Integrity	Reason	400	Understanding	Meaningful	Wise	Abstraction
	Acceptance	350	Forgiveness	Harmonious	Merciful	Transcendence
	Willingness	310	Optimism	Hopeful	Inspiring	Intention
	Neutrality	250	Trust	Satisfactory	Enabling	Release
	Courage	200	Affirmation	Feasible	Permitting	Empowerment
Survival Paradigm	Pride	175	Scorn	Demanding	Indifferent	Inflation
	Anger	150	Hate	Antagonistic	Vengeful	Aggression
	Desire	125	Craving	Disappointing	Denying	Enslavement
	Fear	100	Anxiety	Frightening	Punitive	Withdrawl
	Grief	75	Regret	Tragic	Disdainful	Despondency
	Apathy	50	Despair	Hopeless	Condemning	Abdication
	Guilt	30	Blame	Evil	Vindictive	Destruction
	Shame	20	Humiliation	Miserable	Despising	Elimination

David R. Hawkins MD, PHD, wrote a book titled "The Map of Consciousness Explained" that covers how our bodies operate on an energetic logarithm and each Log has a level that it manifests. The "Map of Consciousness" (google original image) when referenced next to color image of the Chakras will suggest that the levels are color-coded. Knowledge is power, the brain we have is a learning computer- whatever you tell it, it assimilates. The more negative you throw in, the more negative comes out. You are actively programming your brain whether you know you're doing it or not. Negative self-talk (I'm so stupid, I hate my life, etc.) only serve to further strengthen the negative wings of your enneagram. An activity I do is whenever I negative self-talk; I stop and say "I'm not (whatever I said)", "I'm actually (the opposite)", then a positive affirmation. An example is; "I'm sorry I messed up, I'm so stupid. No, I'm not stupid. I'm actually quite smart. I've read many books and demonstrated understanding in many situations." As you can see, the emotional filtered voltage in ME (the author of this book) isn't constantly pegged at max, it does fluctuate negative but I have to overcome that energy. This is my goal for all of us; to modulate our energy to only good. Remember, you cannot fill from an empty pitcher nor can you drink from a dry well- care for yourself first. When you are brimming with positive energy, then you can offer freely but only until the well dips to a comfortable level. You must allow your well to refill- that takes time and not constantly drawing from it.

This rectifying and filtering of energy is your Third Lesson

Notes:

_____

_____

_____

_____

_____

_____

_____

_____

_____

_____

_____

_____

_____

CHAPTER VII

§

YIN/YANG

BEFORE YOU GO ANY FURTHER, you MUST fully understand the Enneagram to keep going. If you don't understand it, most of my notes will "look like Hieroglyphics or Greek"; both places the Enneagram surfaced in its travels. The reason is this is the spiritual third of us, if the MBTI was the Head space and Enneagram was the Heart space, the Yin/Yang relationship is how to interpret and use the information that you intake. It's our instrument panel and viewscreen. It is also insight to all of OUR "cosmic lessons."

The classic Yin (feminine) and Yang (masculine) is the concept/idea/artwork upon which I want to challenge your perspective. In my understanding, we each have our origin (Yin) and our drive (Yang). In my case, my Mother is a 4w3 (Artistic Performer) Yang and 1w2 Yin (Reforming Giver). I am a 5w6 (Conformist Student) Yang and a 2w3 Yin (Motivating Helper-hence the book you are reading).

In times of stress (red arrow on Faces of God), my Mother's Yang 4 goes to 2 (worst self, needs space) and her Yin 1 goes to 4 (dark and moody). She has the natural down-wings of type 5: Detached, absent minded, very self-controlled, and type 9: Huge self-image, procrastinator, cursed with sloth. She has the proclivity to descend into her own deep well and sometimes lash out emotionally from it. If I returned that negative energy (as is easy to do), I would respond with type 4: dramatic, destructive and maudlin energy, and type 1: people-pleasing, absolutism, needing to be the best. When my Yin 2 is unhealthy (unstable), it goes to 8 (the passion) and Yang 5 goes to 7 (needs to fill a void). It turns that maudlin energy into a force of change but destructively! I responded to a lack of attention with a bid for attention (good or bad), sometimes aggressively so. My behavior has been one of swearing, large displays of power (attention-seeking behavior), depression, and then ultimately anger. I have struggled with addiction my whole life; every time was to escape negative energy. If I tried to return the higher wings of type 6 and 3 (Loyalist and Motivator), it would be with much difficulty. Imagine that "Indiana", or Dr. Henry Jones Jr., was your professor. He is brilliant, but sneaks out the window of his office to run off on some expedition. How many times will you re-take the class from the beginning?

Let us now look at the good side of this relationship; When relaxed (black arrow on Faces of God), my Mother's Yang 4 goes to 1 (attentive teacher, people pleaser) and her Yin 1 goes to 7 (most positivity, emits joy). She has the natural up-wings of type 2: Presents best self, empathetic, proud, and type 3: natural efficiency, dynamic and motivational. A person of my Yang 5 and Yin 2 would love to learn something new and thrive in the positive reinforcement. I would respond easily with type 6: loyal, conformist, and courageous energy, and type 3: dynamism, seeking a group, driven to success.

My Father is a 6w5 (Loyal Observer) Yang and 2w1 Yin (Helping Perfectionist).

In times of stress, my Father's Yang 6 goes to 3 (conflicted, repress heart energy) and his Yin 2 goes to 8 (lust for life). He has the natural down-wings of type 7: avoidant, eternal child but the most likeable of all types, and type 3: needs to be noticed, driven to succeed. He would indulge in playing softball, golf, and other distractions to escape from the stresses of his work life with games away from my Mother and I. Whenever he presented low energy like that, I was driven to my downside the 4 (some of your own medicine). I found my own distractions to fill my time- mostly negative ones that affected us all. 5w6's do this to everyone- whatever you are doing that they don't like; they will make sure you understand WHY they don't like it. We are both a little somber for a little too long and both fearful 6s. I am at my best when I voice up, when I embrace my counterphobic 6 because the other will only lead to stagnation.

Let us now look at the good side of *this* relationship; When relaxed, my Father's Yang 6 goes to 9 (mediator with focus) and his Yin 2 goes to 4 (flamboyant artist). He has the natural up-wings of type 5: always observing, excited to find a peer to share experiences, and type 1: serenity, attentive teacher. When he teaches me, my Father is calm, collected and has a variety of instructing styles. He taught me many games; baseball, basketball, football, I didn't want to play any of those. He then taught me how to play pool on a 6-foot table, darts, golf, and most of these we enjoy playing together to this day.

I just want to be noticed and appreciated, Freud was right, it's all about the Mother/Father dynamic. If you are HONEST with yourself, your Yin/Yang is obvious! It's you at your worst and best. Your Yin (Nature) and Yang (Drive) can present in many ways. The Enneagram is the way to control and steer your emotions and thoughts to do what YOU want. If you are able to take a brutal and honest self-assessment (thanks Bill) you will understand your fatal flaw and how to turn it to success. This is the secret to the Force (thanks George).

I have only scratched the surface of the Enneagram in this book. I encourage you to type yourself. Typing others is tricky as you likely don't know as much as you need to for typing and subtyping, but you can know your own self best.

What is your Yin Enneagram?

What is your Yang Enneagram?

Be cognizant of where your types go when unhealthy.

Be aware of the negative behavior you exude.

What positive aspects can you aspire to daily?

CHAPTER VIII

OUR PAINFUL PATH

WAS BORN CATHOLIC SO I read the Bible, Greek and Roman legends, the Book of Mormon, a translated Torah, books on the Quran, Hinduism, and Taoism as well as historic stories of rural cultures. There are many similarities. They have with similar messages but deviate for pointed or avoidant means; We are ALL part of God, we are all connected AS God, treat each other with love and respect, protect yourself by soundly ending any fight, you WILL occasionally fail to meet our expectations but we will forgive you if you show contrition.

Earlier, I presented the concept that this has all been discovered and forgotten, only to be rediscovered then forgotten or hidden. When I realized that, I made the statement; I had to become a Sith so that I could redeem and ascend to a Jedi. <u>I came to this knowledge in fear, anger and suppressed hatred- it led to my suffering, but then understanding was my relief.</u> I am a Grey Jedi, because in my altruism I desire to cultivate and promulgate positive chi, however when pressed I can allow myself to embody the demons of scripture- but I will need to recenter afterward. Walking this line is hard as I am loath to allow myself to lower my vibrations and I do not suggest it as it is almost never necessary. It is easy to fall to the "dark side", one must treat it as a shark in the water you are swimming. It IS present, it will take what it wants if you let it. Proper preparation and execution will keep you safe. The less you distance yourself from the Dark Shark, the more it wants to consume parts of you and leave you bleeding out in the water. The Jedi refused to learn about the Dark Shark or Sith studies for fear it would pull a young mind uncontrollably away so they metaphorically "stay above the water", and this is why they failed- the gigantic blind spot that everything under them could plainly see through. If you can turn back before you fall as deeply as I have, then the Dark Shark doesn't have a taste for you yet and will not chase you as vehemently as it hunts me. Embracing my joy; singing, dancing, exercising, writing, building, these are what makes me happy. This is how I can smile through pain. Hardships are part of life, how you handle them determines if you weaken or strengthen because of these trials.

One who harnesses energy for selfish purposes is the classic Sith and this is what we have in power across most of the Globe. If anyone who sought power maintained their distance from selfishness, they were outnumbered and disappeared. They don't understand what they do because they are broken or they DO understand the repercussions of their actions and simply don't care- these are the scandalous ones. We know about the loud and wild Sith that are on the fringe, but the quantity of all of them far outnumbers the Altruists that survived bribery, extortion, murder attempts and more. The reason for the Rule of 2 is plain to see in American Democracy- rampant backstabbing and backdoor deals, rich ruling class, we are being bitten away at from all sides in this financial feeding frenzy. Being surrounded by Sith on all sides, they have banded together to (seemingly) fight against each other while actually taking turns wearing the crown. The two-party system is corrupt and should be reformed, but no-one in power wants to fix the dysfunctional system because it pays them well.

-------Political Statement, feel free to skip to next chapter--------------

In my humble opinion, this is the way to fix America;

For each sector: MANUFACTURE/Refinery, TRANSPORTATION of goods and people, Trade/EXCHANGE/Governmental Parties, have at least 3 sources (but ideally 5 or more) of INDEPENDENTLY OWNED companies that are not allowed to have any single individual control influence in any other. This is to prevent hidden or obvious monopolies as the founding fathers intended. Competition between the sources will keep prices to customers (government AND civilian) lower while still requiring quality not to drop, lest sales shift to a competitor.

This is the current problem with the two-party system; lack of competition. Any third party (Green, Libertarian, etc.) starts with no backing, and has to sway support from either; the Devil you know and trust, or the Demon he supposedly hates so you have been programmed to hate as well. The American two-party system has repeatedly led to extremism. This is the same spiral that led to the NAZI (National Socialist) party.

Ignorance of the meanings of nationalism and socialism is what keeps that information from being effective and allows it to be used as a scapegoat;

Nationalism: I LOVE MY COUNTRY! My country is the best and I want to make my country stronger, better overall, and truer to its roots.

Socialism: The means of Manufacture, Transportation and Exchange should be owned and regulated by the community as a whole.

Socialism is the basis for a Republic: a state in which supreme power (Regulation/ Exchange) is held by the people through their elected representatives, and which has an elected or nominated president rather than a monarch.

We are a Democratic Republic, because Democracy is a system of government by the WHOLE population or all the eligible members of a state, through elected REPRESENTATIVES.

Those Representatives have been bought out, not all of them but enough to sway any vote in a special interest's desire. The special interests are the top 10% that the bottom 60% of America hates. The middle 30% are those doing just enough to think they are elevating their position, but unless they have a lucky break, they will never get into the top 10%. The bottom half of America is split between; "I love my country, we need to fix the problems, don't infringe on MY RIGHTS", and then "Let the government figure it out, there are programs to help, if we all give a little, we all get a lot", I'm willing to sacrifice freedoms for protection.

Our problem is that the people at the top have bought out our share of representation and know that with only two parties, there are always enough people at the bottom to balance or sometimes overpower the votes of the people in the middle 30%. As long as the lower class can be swayed to vote in your favor, you can stay in power.

This is why we lose, because the majority lacks options and accurate representation. Seriously consider a third-party candidate for elected offices, it could fix America. "But it will split the votes from MY GUY!" If the votes come out 35%, 34%, and 31% with a 2% margin of error- I would understand the need for a recount. We already have recounts that the American wage-earner has to pay for in the end through the Elections Official using your collected taxes. The system has been modified to be divisive and it's very good at it.

If you likewise wish to become; a Jedi, an Altruist, or "the change in the world you wish to see", then this is the book for you. The path is painful, but the reward is infinite.

CHAPTER IX

OODA LOOP

WHEN I WAS IN HIGH school, I took Air Force JROTC class instead of gym because, I HATED gym. The running, the sports, all of it. (5w6 empowered in 8 exhibiting 9). One of the instructors was an F4 Phantom pilot in Vietnam and afterwards. He explained how while flying at hundreds of miles per hour, He was able to constantly identify targets and eliminate them- There was a process developed by military strategist Col. John Boyd (USAF): the OODA Loop.

Observe and Orient: Find your location, mission status, and threats.

Decide (on a Course of Action or CoA): Using the acquired information,

determine your next action or series of actions.

Act: Perform the determined action(s) to the fullest of your ability.

...repeat

This is what ties it all together for me;

1) Observe the energy being exhibited at me

2) Center yourself to utilize the observation <u>dispassionately</u> and decide to exhibit the <u>upper wings</u> of my yin and yang

3) Act in the matter with Love and Humility

    a. Return to step 1

This can be done on the interpersonal level in a conversation.

It can be hourly or daily; I build lists of things I need to get done that day and check things off as completed.

It can be weekly or monthly for larger tasks, in this case- stage the tasks in the order they need to be completed. One example could be to pick the location of a vacation, then buy tickets. After the trip dates are secured, you can look at the weather, and following that plan an itinerary. Once all of this is done, only then can you pack with the knowledge of where you are going, the planned activities, and the likely weather in the area. It seems like a lot, but taken one step at a time- it helps ME. You may be different.

How does this combine with all of the spirituality we have been discussing? Look at the artwork on the cover and next page, the three comets are the OODA Loop, as well as the flow of energy in each of the states

- Capture the situation (Spiritual) Heart- Take no action in your imbalance

- Determine a CoA (Intellectual) Head- Center Yourself and find a path

- Act-(Physical) Body- Align yourself in the direction chosen

Inside each of the comets is a pair of Yin-Yang symbols. Notice the comet at the top; the energy is equally distributed between the two symbols, they appear even and centered- This is the time to decide, when you are centered and at peace. Notice the comet

to the bottom right; the energy is fully at the front being pushed by one Yin-Yang, there

is energy flowing between the other Yin-Yang

but less and they are connected-This is the

time to act, when you have decided on a clear

course of action, pay no attention to the other

options. Notice the comet to the bottom left;

the energy is unequal and pushing away from

center, the Yin-Yang symbols are diagonal and

out of alignment-This is the time to NOT take

action and instead simply <u>observe</u>.

When you need to decide something, close this book and align the comet at the top

to point away from you, the energy at the center should point to you and to the path

directly ahead of you. Where are the pips in the Yin-Yang? They are level, as are all the

other pips in the other comets, but the other Yin-Yang symbols look out of balance! It's

your perspective.

When you have your course of action determined, rotate the book artwork so that

you have the comet for action pointing so that the Yin-Yang symbols are aligned pointing

from you to the path ahead. Where are the pips on the Yin-Yang symbols now? The pips

in your comet seem out of balance, but trust in the path you have chosen. The pips in the

other comets appear in disarray as well, and their Yin-Yang symbols seem out of balance

from this perspective.

When the action has been completed, rotate the book artwork as close as you can to

aligning the comet in a path directly ahead of you. It will be difficult to do if not impossi-

ble because the entire comet is out of alignment. Notice how there is so much energy from the "action" comet in alignment, and how your comet's energy is disparate and uneven. Nothing seems in balance, you should make no decisions and take no actions, simply observe the chaos around you.

By this point you might see that we are all independently operating in this cycle whether consciously or not and at different positions in the cycle. From each perspective, the yin-yang symbols and their pips seemingly came into and out of alignment but the artwork itself NEVER changed. **This is the lesson**- center yourself and keep your perspective before taking any action, lest you fall to your lesser, easier path and behave Demonically lest you be cast into your own personal Hell. Some people mentally count to 10 in stressful situations to help them re-center and decide how to best act. There is another YouTube video by "The Shaolin Way" titled, "Dichotomy of Control – Shaolin Masters Shi Heng Yi talks Epictetus", in which the Master discusses the internal versus external self, as well as the individual interacting with the community. He discusses "Qigong" or breath-work, and this is our sine wave, when hyperventilating, the body can get light-headed or faint. When exercising, singing or meditating the breath finds a natural rhythm. This sine wave started when you were born, regulates your heart rate and ceases upon death. It's also the basis for any Astrology, your sine wave is tuned to a specific seasonal vibration, what you choose to attenuate to it determines your life.

If you understand all that I have presented here, then you have worked toward opening your Third-Eye Chakra and are on the way to accessing your Crown Chakra. This is the time that you will be tested the most, but will be able to see most things clearly. Continue your work until the act of personifying both wings of your Enneagram identity positively comes to you easily and naturally.

There are guided meditations online that help. If you googled the terms and watched the videos then you primed the algorithm for spirituality and they will stay in your feed as long as you watch those videos. Once you started the process of enlightenment, you have allowed the energy to flow up to the higher Chakra, and you are on the way to accessing the greater God that we ALL are, but that energy is powerful and much sought after by others- protect Your energy. Yoga and meditation will help elevate your Chi/energy/ vibration. Once you can access the Crown Chakra, you ARE enlightened and the secrets of the Universe are open to you. Congratulations! Remember that energy is always in flux and it will be easier to let yourself take the lower path of least resistance but it will drain or foul your energy well.

This final "Pursuit of Balance" has been your Last Lesson from Me; If you can master this balance in yourself and work towards balance with those around you, then you are a <u>beginning</u> Yogi, Guru, Rabbi or Teacher and are now able to continue your journey as well as assist others in their journey, but remember to maintain YOUR balance. In "Star Wars" terms, you have been granted the promotion from Youngling to Padawan (you have access to knowledge enough to the point of being dangerous). Who you choose to draw your information and growth from is directly determinate of your path. Altruism is key in life; If we all work towards the greater good while keeping our own well being in mind then society, as a whole, stands to benefit.

How do we act "altruistically" in a world of negativity? For each of us, we have to choose our specific reactions. I have listed a few examples in the next chapter of the first few times I was able to consciously attempt this. The lesson I am still learning is when to withdraw from the situation as this has always been presented to me as a defeat, but sometimes "discretion is the better part of valor", in more plain-speak; "pick your battles". Many of the things I have presented here have been said in many other ways, so I have attempted to tie them all together in a coherent package. As Master Shi Heng Yi said, control yourself first, your stress arises from inside yourself and is only triggered by external stimuli. One of the most important messages about minding your own faults over those of others comes from the Bible;

> "Why do you notice the splinter in your brother's eye, but do not perceive the wooden beam in your own? How can you say to your brother, 'Brother, let me remove that splinter in your eye,' when you do not even notice the wooden beam in your own eye?" Matthew 7: 3-5

CHAPTER X

USING IT ALL TOGETHER

THE FIRST TIME I WAS successful at consciously channeling negative energy, my "fight or flight reaction" was triggered by my Mother exhibiting the downside of 5 (Absent-minded detachment) and downside of 9 (Huge Ego) by making statements or performing actions that she knows irritate me because <u>I have asked her in the past to not do them</u>. I cannot properly heal (emotionally or physically) when the wound is not safe from re-injury. My natural (easiest) reaction is exhibiting the downside of the 1 (attention seeking) and the downside of the 4 (Dramatic) combined with a counterphobic 6. The last time she violated my wishes, I had gotten angry and made a display of that anger to which she exhibited the downward side of 5 (withdrawn) and 1 (no energy). The event was unhealthy, no progress was made and no one felt good about anything- not even me after screaming and crying about "the emotional pain she was causing me." By allowing this negative energy to spiral downward I hurt my Mother: the woman who gave me life. Since the pattern has re-emerged, my hands began to physically tremble because I knew what <u>could</u> happen. I collected myself and looked at my options. I then exhibited the upside of the 2 (Humility) and the upside of the 6 (courage) with the counterphobic 6 (as I am naturally a phobic 6). I took a breath, looked at my mother, and asked her again not to repeat this behavior: "[This] is specifically the thing that is triggering me. You are hurting me, your son. Please stop." I did it without tears, monotone, slowly but with focus on Her. She chose her typical reaction of shutting down, but I was able to convey my feelings. Typically, after shutting down, I don't see her again for two days. This time we had lunch together 5 hours after the event. I love you, Mom!

Another time (same day) I was at my aunt's house and talking about these discoveries I had that I was writing a book about, exhibiting positive energy 5w6 (courage) and 2w3 (integrity). This cousin of mine has long been spiritual and I wanted to pick her brain and see if she had any new leads for me to add to the book and help my understanding. Her response was one of jaded skepticism. Because I had just come home and haven't been close to the family for a while, I didn't understand how to address this. We continued, me pouring out good energy, asking for her to tell me what she believes in, what works for her, what brought her peace. She continued returning complaints and examples of pain-negative energy. My other cousin walked out to the porch and without a word, physically stumbled away from both of us. He said that the energies coming out of there were intense and he wanted none of it. We continued talking for a while and she became more avoidant and conflicted. Referencing the love cards chapter, I am a 9 of hearts; Universal Love- I interpret this to mean that I am a strong font of positive energy. We are all wells of energy, some more full than others. The thing is, a well can run dry from being too heavily used or contaminated from some skeleton or other crap thrown in. In this case, my cousin was a powerful well of energy (chi) but she has something festering in there. She has learned to get used to the foul taste and thinks that this is all there could be. When she found a pure well, she tried to dump some of her "fouled water" in there. Because I have done the work of draining the well, dropping down into it and removing all the "corpses of past sins" and learned how to properly channel my energy(chi). Every time she dumped some out, I flooded more good energy out there. At the end, her well was dry, I left the place and told her to have an awesome day (a little good energy to try to fill the well). I Love you, Cuz!

[You asked for examples, you became one]

In both situations, I approached with my higher side (my higher wings). The positive wing 3 of my yin was; Integrity, dynamism, competence in real life, natural leader. The positive wing 6 of my yang was; Courage, loyal, curiosity. The second time (with my cousin), it happened naturally. Only now in my analysis and citation of the event will I look at the downside that I could have exhibited: negative traits of 1 and 4: resentment, people pleasing, maudlin, tragic gives them energy, needs to be special. This is a dangerous combination. Only now in the analysis do I realize that this is what happened to her: she met someone else so damaged that they poisoned her well and she got used to it. She tried (unconsciously) to poison my well, but I said Nah.

Cousin, I will give you a first edition print of this and pray it helps.

Now, let us examine a time that I FAILED; It is important for you to understand that even though I LITERALLY wrote the book on how to project good energy out, even I can still fail.

A group of 8 of us had just finished playing a round of golf and were hungry, so we went to an adjacent restaurant for a late lunch. Two of us arrived before the main party and when we told them we had a group of 8- they told us that they couldn't seat us until the entire party was present. I accepted that at face value and proceeded to busy myself by observing the decorations. There was a large table of 16 or so people in the middle of the dining area, but it was after 1pm so I expected there to be table space. Our party began to trickle in and after 15 minutes we were all present. Only then did the two greeters begin assembling a table. They wanted to seat all 8 large men at two small square tables pushed together right next to the party of 16 that was taking up four large tables. I began wiping off the crumbs from the last meal eaten at these tables ("We can wipe down the tables" she said but didn't perform) and moving the chairs around to bring in a third table when they said, "you can't have that table too". I then explained that we would need more room than they had allotted us for the plates and drinks. They said "We just can't do it!". This was my breaking point; after watching them kill time on their phones when they could have been assembling a table, after accepting dismissal from a service industry that is not wiping down the tables between customers, and then after being told that we would not be allowed a third table after lunchtime in an almost empty room, I lost my cool and said: "Fuck all this bullshit, I'm fucking done!" and left the restaurant. I held the door for other patrons on the way out, but I was in the wrong in my reaction.

What happened? I had spent so much of myself golfing and having a good time but that isn't how my Enneagram 5 recovers energy- I like seclusion and isolation. My enneagram 2 was trying to be helpful by speeding up the preparation of the table but my help was rebuffed. I was low on energy, and my attempt to regain some was met with bad energy. In this low energy state, I succumbed to the lower self; I allowed my enneagram 8 (boss) energy fuel my 7 (vulgarity) and out came derision and contempt. Were they in the wrong? YES. Was I in the wrong? YES.

What could I have done instead?

1) Calmly ask the greeter why we weren't allowed to have a third small table for a party of 8 when the party of 16 had four large ones. Make an attempt to reason with them. (Best move)

2) Ask if this is how they typically treat customers here, and if the manager is present (the "Karen" move)

3) Ask for the owner's number to call and lodge a complaint (rarely successful).

4) Simply stated that this is unacceptable treatment and left the restaurant. (Second best move)

I was already depleted, and the low response has long been my reaction in my sickness so it is WELL developed. This is probably true for many readers of this book, but the truth is- you can turn it around.

I had a therapist tell me that "you can un-learn skills" when talking about reactive defensiveness. I tried to explain to him that you can't UN-learn things but you can "counter-train" opposing skills to overcome the problem, but his mind was closed so I will present this argument here; When you learn in infancy that blue, red, and yellow make a variety of colors from brown to orange to purple, dependent upon the quantities of each in the mix. You know that it's a FACT because you have confirmed it manually as a child. What would you say if I told you that they make black instead? When talking in terms of light, cyan, magenta and yellow light traps in series catches all the light of the rainbow from the light source and made black! This is because of the colors combined "reflectance" or how much of a given wavelength each pigment reflects. The light source would only see a brighter white light, so from their perspective, it gets brighter white, not black.

Learning skills in new fields is like training a new muscle group for the first time- the initial few sets of reps hurt. The more consistently you do it, the easier it gets. I am not saying it is ever easy- it is a lifelong struggle, but one that makes you a better person and the world around you a better place to live.

MY SPECIFIC snap-to low response is *ANGER*, I've become very good at channeling my disapproval into biting verbal attacks as well as been trained to ground-fight to the death. Long ago, before I started studying most of this, I overcame my road rage in a weird way. I had a geriatric cat that my then wife had brought into the marriage. She didn't always make it to the cat-box, sometimes she threw up food she ate too fast or clawed me when she fell. I used to massage her legs that were failing, I'd protect her from the aggressive kitten, give her the best pets and make her purr (for an hour or so while watching tv) when she sat on my chest. I loved on her and kept her alive longer than the veterinarian expected, but one of the times I was cleaning after her, I was angrily griping about it and stood up from a crouch to look her in the eyes (as she was of course supervising the cleanup) and her face seemed to say to me; "I'm sorry, I can't help it." Then as now typing this, I teared up... I had been venting venom at this pet who now had ME as her whole world. I immediately kissed her head and loved on her, then I went back to finish cleaning up and gave the cats fresh food and water. There were four cats at this time and I was unemployed. I was unhappy with my career path, my marriage, my finances- and these are the times I have grown emotionally and spiritually, in times of great pain and suffering. Returning to road rage; I thought that if every time I got upset that someone was driving "not how I think they should," I would then imagine that my grandmother, who passed while I was deployed to Afghanistan, was behind the wheel. I couldn't be mad at grandma! (If your family dynamic is different, I apologize, please choose another "Patronus" (The Patronus Charm, introduced in Harry Potter and the Prisoner of Azkaban, is a defensive spell which produces a silver, animal guardian, used to protect a witch or wizard against Dementors).

This worked as long as I applied the practice- when I stopped envisioning my grandma, I raged again. The band-aid had fallen off and I was "bleeding on people who didn't hurt me." My base problem is ANGER, so what defeats anger? Why did "my grandmother" work as a band-aid for rage? I think that gratitude defeats anger for ME (downsides 2w1

Reformer, 5w4 Artist); If someone approaches you shouting that you threw your trash in their trash can and seems agitated beyond a reasonable level and you responded with gratitude instead of defensive anger the result changes. "I'm sorry, thank you for telling me- I will make sure not to do it (whether you did it or not)". There can be no fight when you give space to anger, and to thank them on top of that would just mystify them long enough for you to walk away. Gratitude is hard, but given perspective it gets easier: I'm typing this on a laptop I purchased with money I made contracting for the government. I served in the military and was trained in a useful trade, had loving parents and did not grow up in a warzone. As I type this, Ukraine is a nation of cities reduced to smoking rubble, families displaced or split. There are millions living homeless while I type on my couch that I paid for when I sold one of my businesses. Given perspective, gratitude is easy, but it's even easier to not gain perspective- which is how I fail.

What is your low-side behavior? What gets YOU in trouble?

What pours water on the flames? How can YOU help yourself?

I'm typing all of this, you've read this far- it's easy to say and understand, but putting it into practice takes effort and focus. Like I said earlier, this path is not easy, but it IS rewarding. On top of the good feelings, there is a physical aspect to all of this. Negative reactions, negative thinking, it all stresses our hearts. Our bodies are all chemical power generators turning potential energy in carbs and proteins into new body cells and electrical energy. The more positive energy you harness and bless others with, the more at peace and serene you feel. The more negative energy you collect and emit, the more metaphorical "force lightning" you send through your heart. I am eschewing that negativity because I have lived in it, on and off, for decades- my days are limited.

It is important for you to understand that even though you have read all of this and may even understand and practice it- we are still fallible. There will come a time where you will not act appropriately, we ALL can experience that. It is best for us all to give you the space you need to heal whatever hurt you and go on with our day. The "Cosmic We" (the Collective God, made of all of us lesser Gods) forgive you for being Human, please learn from this failure and ascend even higher. Once ascended, you will more easily act Angelic.

This is a life-long goal, and I personally believe that the biblical Armageddon is simply each of our own deaths. You will panic at least a little at the end but if your Angels and those who love you out-weigh your Demons (those you despise and who despise you back), then your passing may be somewhat relieved by the physical presence of those angels you "Begat". If not, then the room is empty and filled only with thoughts of what we should have done and who we wished was there "one last time". Those passed elders that you knew in life are in the memories of them flooding back as you relive your life one last time as you are confined to the temple that is "your body" for "your sins". My cousin recently passed from cancer, but He swore that he saw many of his elders from his youth just before he left us.

I love you, all of you- <u>even the bad parts</u> (that's the start)

POST SCRIPT

Typing this manual, I feel so positive and productive. This book was finished January 6th and then we (my parents, the editors and first critics-at my request, of this book) had a feast where we all ate bread and I ate fish with my pitcher of water. We just left "Epiphany Mass". I think that meal may have been on the same cosmic day that Jesus had The Last Supper. I'm naturally concerned about the crucifixion that is therefore coming, but I will weather the storm, or I won't- I won't worry about the future until it becomes the present. While this "beaming" feeling is present, I understand that the opposite is possible and the more I think about ANYTHING, the more into the present it comes.

In this effort, I try to act towards my positive ends 2w3 and 5w6 while eschewing the aspects of my disturbed state 7. While I do that, I try to embody my healthy state 8 and acting in the POSITIVE ASPECTS ONLY of my dramatic artist 4 and perfectionist reformer 1. To translate that into plain-speak: I try to be a motivating giver and a faithful observer by leading people and believing that art relieves angst. Meaning: I'm writing this book for whoever needs help in a dark place, it is also my way of giving back to those who helped me. I pray that by reading the contents, applying them to ourself, and discussing it, we can embody a more-healthy society.

Thank you for reading this far, now I encourage you to read the book again and write in <u>pencil</u> wherever you feel compelled, including the cover. The reason I emphasize in pencil is because life is fluid, things change. Before I was reborn last time, I was so close to having everything I ever wanted; a fiancée, a son in college and a newborn daughter, I had proven myself in many areas. Then a series of mistakes cost me everything, I thought I had it figured out- but I was wrong. You WILL be wrong sometimes just as I will be wrong again- this is the PURSUIT of balance. <u>It never ends.</u> This copy is then YOUR book, add to its wisdom however you feel inclined. You will probably realize things you missed earlier, or have additional testimony to inscribe. As you have time to make this YOUR book and collect your notes, it will become your user manual to the point you no longer need it.

I then also encourage you to give your written-in manual to someone that you love, that is **deeply** in need of help. You could purchase another to re-read and write in as you wish- this small act of kindness (good karma) is sure to come back to you somehow, some way. I personally have had a wondrous life across lush mountains, fertile fields, desert vistas, and months at sea. There were several occasions where a hummingbird or butterfly circles me for a few minutes then flies off. My mind springs to Jeff Dayton- "Flutter-by, Butterfly" and I encourage you to YouTube it. I met him at Ward's Rafters in Waikiki when I was working In Hawaii. BIG Mahalo to Maggie for taking me and encouraging me to go out when on Oahu- a truly magical isle.

Aloha 'Oe- *Dio the Phoenix*

Printed in the United States
by ▢▢ker & Taylor Publisher Services